Reforming the U.S. Supreme Court

Norman Black

Books by Norman Black

Combat Veterans' Stories of World War II
Volume 1, North Africa and Europe
Volume 2, Pacific, China, Burma

Combat Veterans' Stories of the Korean War
(Two volumes)

Combat Veterans' Stories of the Vietnam War
(Five volumes)

Combat Veterans' Stories of Small Wars and Nation Building
(Three Volumes)

Ice, Fire, and Blood a novel of the Korean War

Combat Veterans Returned with PTSD and TBI

The cover photo shows the statue of "Lady Justice", which stands in front of the Augusta-Richmond County Judicial Center, in Augusta, Georgia. This representation of Justice is not blindfolded, in order for her to use all her senses to weigh facts in legal cases.

Photo by Tina Monaco of Augusta, Georgia

This document was prepared for publication by Rinat Bikineyev of Rockville, Maryland.

Copyright © 2022 Norman Black

All rights reserved

Content

Introduction 1

The problem 1

Examples 11

Reform 25

Summary 29

Reforming the U.S. Supreme Court

Introduction

This document discusses problems, which the U.S. Supreme Court presents to stability and democracy in the United States. It then gives examples of the problem and concludes with recommendations about how to depoliticize the Court.

The problem

The U.S. Supreme Court has made itself the senior legislative body of the United States' government. Originally, its legitimacy came from faithfully interpreting laws passed by Congress and adhering to the Constitution that is the foundational governing document of the country, as amended. For decades, the Court's behavior has been a usurpation of legislative and executive branch power.

Article three, section two, of the U.S. Constitution specifies the Supreme Court's jurisdiction, thusly: "The judicial Power shall extend to all Cases, in Law and Equity, arising under this Constitution, the Laws of the United States, and Treaties made, or which shall be made, under their Authority;—to all Cases affecting Ambassadors, other public Ministers and Consuls;—to all Cases of admiralty and maritime Jurisdiction;—to Controversies to which the United States shall be a Party;—to Controversies between two or more States;—between a State and Citizens of another State,—between Citizens of different States,— between Citizens of the same State claiming Lands under Grants of different States, and between a State, or the Citizens thereof, and foreign States, Citizens or Subjects."

The Court's right to review U.S. laws is not a right granted it by the Constitution. In 1803, by ruling in Marbury v. Madison, the Court gave itself the extra-legal right to strike down presidential and congressional acts. The case created the doctrine of Judicial Review. John Marshall, the contemporary Chief Justice, said the right was implied in the Constitution, and that some state high courts ruled on conformity of their states' laws with their state constitutions. Marshall's implementation of this judicial review meant judicial supremacy, which has remained in effect since.

Marshall got away with his power grab, apparently because the other federal branches expected that Supreme Court rulings would be based upon principle and not upon justices' preferences or prejudices.

Unfortunately, the Court has been inconsistent in what it has decreed is law. Since the U.S. was founded, the Supreme Court has reversed its own decisions more than 300 times. It has also taken rights from states and centralized them in the federal government.

During the 1800s, the Court's decisions attempted to balance federal power with state sovereignty. The Court occasionally found new, constitutional reasons why it could rule on state laws, but it mainly avoided ruling on matters not enumerated in the Constitution. However, in 1857, it involved itself in dispute about slavery and property rights and handed down the Dred Scott decision.

Today, law schools in the U.S. teach that the U.S. Constitution is what the U.S. Supreme Court says it is. The unelected Supreme Court and federal appeals courts' judges have made the judiciary the dominant branch of U.S. governance. The Supreme Court strikes down or re-writes laws enacted by elected Congresses, and signed by elected presidents. Their sovereignty is a danger to representative government.

The creation of new law by the Supreme Court has developed gradually. The present republic began in 1789, after the U.S. constitution was ratified the previous year. The new constitution divided power between the new federal government and the states. The federal government had three theoretically equal governmental branches: legislative, executive, and judicial. The states that created the new governing document already had their constitutions, which continued in effect. To prevent the federal government from infringing on the rights of states' citizens, Congress adopted ten amendments, in 1791. These amendments are known as the Bill of Rights. They forbid the federal government to infringe upon personal freedoms and rights of states' citizens, limit the federal government's rights in judicial and other proceedings, and clearly state that all powers not specifically granted to the federal government by the Constitution belong to the states or the people.

The Court was not created to be an unelected über-legislature. It digressed from the role assigned it by the Constitution and has become the supreme U.S. legislative branch. It arrogates legislative power to itself, strikes down laws, and rewrites laws and regulations to suit the will of its contemporary members. As a result, it has become highly political and contentious.

The founders expected that the judicial branch of the U.S. government would be the least dangerous for representative democracy. However, the Supreme Court's members have repeatedly given themselves the power to decide issues that rightfully belong to Congress and the president. They have thereby made those elected branches largely impotent.

Appointing members of the Court has become an important way to influence Court decisions. Any president that can name several members to the Court can ensure that his political views become a legacy, which continues to dominate Court decisions long after his term in office ends.

Litigants before the Court want judicial activism, when their case before the Court requires that the Court make new law, as compared with interpreting it. Their opponents want judicial restraint if it serves their position.

In the 1950s, the Court became very assertive, and has since handed down decisions that have negated or rewritten many laws and regulations. Supreme Court decisions that legislate are now so frequent and important that many voters consider who a presidential candidate might nominate for a vacant seat on the Court, before voting for that presidential candidate.

One problem with appointments to Federal courts is that judges on them are appointed for life by presidents, with the Senate's advice and consent. Voters have no say in this procedure. Once appointed, U.S. judges are free to include their individual prejudices and preferences in their legal decisions. They are also free to review state and federal laws, regulations, and presidential orders and declare them unconstitutional. Since World War II, the Court has not limited its jurisdiction to clarifying constitutional points, but has ruled on social and political subjects.

Today, the record and thinking of potential candidates for the Court are so thoroughly investigated, before they are nominated, that appointees' decisions seldom disappoint the president that appointed them. Potential nominees' writing, rulings, and speeches are reviewed to try to ensure that when a nominee is on the Court his (or her) judicial decisions will support that president's political views.

When justices' votes in controversial cases can be predicted before a case is considered by them, then constitutional law is pure partisan politics. This has gradually become the situation. As a result, the Court is now an extension of political power, and represents the party that placed the majority on it.

Senate confirmation hearings of nominees have become unpleasant political events because the justices have given themselves the right to consider and resolve matters, which Congress was designed to resolve. During those hearings, persons nominated to the Court evade giving direct answers and sometimes lie, in order to win approval of their nominations.

Once on the Court, the justices have virtually complete control of which cases they hear. They often intervene in cases just because they see an opportunity to change a law. The Court is not subject to any checks on the cases it decides to hear or the legislation that it nullifies or re-writes. In doing so, they have become political partisans. Congress can theoretically impeach the justices, or add members to the Court. Neither of these actions has yet been taken, regardless of how activist the Court has been.

Court appointees have handed down decisions that alter or nullify federal and state laws and regulations not in accord with the Court's members. The result is that the Court has legislative power superior to that of the Congress. The justices of the U.S. Supreme Court have for decades overturned U.S. and state laws and regulations and forbidden presidential orders and thus subverted the roles of U.S. presidents and Congresses.

Congressional candidates seldom run for office on a promise to enact a politically divisive law, which could be repealed after the next election. However, if one can get a Supreme Court decision, which makes new law through interpreting an existing one, that is far easier than striving to have a Congress and president enact that law. As a result, the nation's most difficult issues are decided by the Court, and the nation's Congress and president are bypassed.

Until the 1900s, the Court declared U.S. laws unconstitutional five times. By 1950, the Court declared about one law unconstitutional during each presidential term. By the 1990's, the Court declared three or four laws unconstitutional during each presidential term. This increase happened because the Court became willing to be at the center of political and social questions. It now lacks respect for the elected branches of government and does not hesitate to step in and negate or change laws and executive branch regulations.

The great increase in the Court's activity has resulted in it overturning more than three hundred of its own decisions. One result is that the public recognizes that the justices are political partisans. Another is legal instability, which is not good for representative democracy.

The Constitution, in Article Three, gives the federal judiciary the power to handle cases or controversies arising under federal law, federal treaties, controversies involving multiple states or foreign powers, when ambassadors, public officials, if the states are a party in the case, and other enumerated areas. The Constitution does not grant the federal judiciary the power to rule on the constitutionality of U.S. laws or to rule on the constitutionality of state laws, except when multiple states are involved in a case.

The Court's most outrageous addition to its power to review laws is its inclusion of the first eight amendments to the Constitution in its purview.

The first 10 amendments, called the Bill of Rights, were added to the Constitution in order to specifically guarantee personal freedoms and rights, place clear limitations on the U.S. government's power in judicial and other proceedings, and explicitly declare that all powers not specifically delegated to Congress by the Constitution are reserved for the states or the people. These amendments did not apply to state laws, which were governed by state constitutions.

These ten amendments are in the Constitution because many of the founding fathers feared that the federal government would usurp these rights. When enacted, it was clearly understood that these amendments applied only to the federal government and to federal court cases. They forbid the U.S. government from legislating about, or encroaching on, the rights protected by these amendments. By ratifying these amendments, the States meant to permanently remove civil rights mentioned in them from federal jurisdiction.

The Supreme Court's march to legislating and overturning U.S. and state laws and regulations developed slowly. The greatest subversion of the Constitution happened during the Progressive Era, as the Court gradually gave itself the right to rule in matters related to the Bill of Rights. It granted itself this power by deciding that the Due Process Clause of the Fourteenth Amendment trumps the fact that the first ten amendments were ratified to prevent the U.S. government from legislating about subjects named in those ten amendments.

The Court began this process on the basis of several sentences in the 14th amendment, which say, "No State shall make or enforce any law which shall abridge the privileges or immunities of citizens of the United States; nor shall any state deprive any person of life, liberty, or property, without due process of law; nor deny to any person within its jurisdiction the equal protection of the law."

Using these sentences as justification, the Supreme Court, ruled that the federal Bill of Rights applies to State governments as well as to the federal government. This Court ruling is called the "incorporation doctrine". With gross disregard for the Founders' purpose, the Supreme Court has gradually ruled that these amendments restrict the States as well as the federal government. In this way, the Supreme Court gave itself jurisdiction over the laws and regulations of every State.

Before the Court included the Bill of Rights in its jurisdiction, it was acknowledged in Congresses and by Supreme Courts that the Bill of Rights applied only to the U.S. government and federal court cases. States were not obliged to legislate about these subjects.

On the basis of the Due Process Clause, the Supreme Court ruled, by 1925, that the first eight amendments of the Bill of Rights apply to state governments as well as the federal government. This Court ruling is called the "Incorporation Doctrine". With this ruling, the Supreme Court gave itself jurisdiction over laws and regulations of every State.

In The Federalist, No. 78, Alexander Hamilton foresaw a different role for the Court. He wrote, "Whoever attentively considers the different departments of power must perceive that, in a government in which they are separated from each other, the judiciary, from the nature of its functions, will always be the least dangerous to the political rights of the Constitution; because it will be least in a capacity to annoy or injure them. The Executive not only commands the purse, but holds the sword of the community. The legislature not only commands the purse, but prescribes the rules by which the duties and rights of every citizen are to be regulated. The judiciary, on the contrary, has no influence over either the sword or the purse; no direction either of the strength or of the wealth of the society; and can take no active resolution whatever. It may truly be said to have neither force nor will, but merely judgment..."

Patrick Henry of Virginia played a major part in removing British rule over England's American colonies. He wanted Virginia to be self-governing, but not part of the U.S., for he foresaw northeastern dominance in a political union. When Virginia decided to join the U.S., despite his wish, he worked to ensure that the Constitution was modified by 20 amendments that would protect States' citizens and States from the U.S. Only 12 were presented to Congress and only ten of those were accepted and became constitutional amendments known as the Bill of Rights.

When those first ten amendments to the constitution were submitted to states to ratify, it was understood that they were needed to prevent the U.S. government from encroaching on the rights of states' and their citizens. Their intent is made clear by the First Amendment's initial wording, which is "Congress shall make no law..."

In the years since, the Court has become stronger than Congresses and presidents. This is largely because justices are secure in their positions for life. That gives them great freedom in how they rule and on what laws and regulations they decide to review. That they make decisions on the basis of their opinions is to be expected, for they are mere human beings. Their personal partiality and preferences are reflected in how they discharge their duties. They are also influenced by prestige and power, which accrue to their über-legislature. In U.S. politics, they are the supreme beings.

With no restraints on its activities, the Court has made itself the most important political and social policymaking institution in the U.S. It has legislated policies about education, religion, marriage, morals, law enforcement, welfare, voting, who may use a women's toilet, and other matters reserved by the Constitution to the States. It does this by "judicial review" which is not authorized by the Constitution, but is a power assumed by the Court.

While on the Court, its justices also dispense their views in books, which they write, and as speakers at conventions of lawyers and judges in the U.S. and internationally. They present themselves to audiences as the supreme U.S. adjudicators of the U.S. Constitution: without prejudices, above politics, and squeaky clean politically. Unfortunately, their record contradicts their pretensions.

Abraham Lincoln said that a bad Supreme Court decision can be overturned later by a different Supreme Court. The inconsistent record of Court rulings proves this truism, for the Court has overturned its previous decisions more than 300 times. This happens when new justices are appointed due to retirements and deaths of sitting justices, and the new justice's prejudices or preferences affect Court decisions. That means that what a previous Court deemed wrong, a Court with new justices sometimes deems right.

The public is correct to view the Court as a political organization, when the appointment of new justices to it can change the meaning of laws. These flip-flops in Court decisions are troubling, for stability is a key requirement for representative democracy to thrive.

Partisan justices can hand down decisions that thwart presidential actions and congressional laws. The degree to which they do so undermines the separation of powers described by the Constitution. Unfortunately, there is no check or balance on the Supreme Court, and it and lower federal courts are guilty of accepting cases that are clearly not federal matters.

Congress has proven unable to legislate on many controversial matters. One result is that persons that want laws changed find a legal conflict or part of a law, which may be interpreted their way. They then sue and appeal their cases to the Supreme Court in hope that the highest court will accept their interpretation.

The Court has been willing to adjudicate matters, which are rightly legislative, and to insert itself into whatever it fancies. As a result, when the Court is controlled by conservative judges, conservative interests appeal to it and often get favorable rulings, which enable them to bypass Congress or a state legislature. When liberals control the Court, liberal interests do the same. For example, in 2020,

Amy Coney Barrett, who has many hard right opinions, was appointed to the Court and became the sixth conservative Court justice. In reaction to this situation, liberal advocacy organizations scrapped plans to bring lawsuits, which might eventually result in Supreme Court rulings, which would overturn decisions repulsive to them. Instead, conservative groups began to fashion ways to institute lawsuits, which would eventually reach the Supreme Court and result in decisions favored by them.

Examples

A few examples of inconsistent decisions by the U.S. Supreme Court shall illustrate the Court's inconsistency problem.

In 1833, in Barron v. Maryland, the plaintiff claimed that the right to due process, which is guaranteed by this amendment, applies to state governments as well as to the federal government. The Supreme Court, headed by John Marshall disagreed and said that the amendments only limited the federal government.

Marshall, an extreme nationalist, noted that, "The constitution was ordained and established by the people of the United States for themselves, for their own government, and not for the government of the individual states..." This was a clear statement that none of the restrictions mentioned in the Bill of Rights applied to states; they restricted only to the U.S. government.

In the Slaughterhouse Cases' decision, in 1873, the Court explicitly rejected that the Bill of Rights applied to states. In an attempt to improve sanitary conditions, the Louisiana legislature and the city of New Orleans had created a corporation charged with regulating the slaughterhouse industry. Members of the Butchers' Benevolent Association challenged the constitutionality of the corporation, claiming that it violated the Fourteenth Amendment. That amendment had been ratified in 1868 to protect civil rights of millions of newly freed Negro slaves, but the Butchers claimed that the amendment protected their right to "sustain their lives through labor".

The Court held that the Fourteenth Amendment protected only those rights guaranteed by the U.S.: it did not restrict the police powers of Louisiana. The Court stated that it was not the purpose of the Fourteenth Amendment "to bring within the power of Congress the entire domain of civil rights heretofore belonging exclusively to the states".

In 1876, in United States v. Cruikshank, the Court ruled that the First and Second Amendments did not apply to states or private persons, despite wording in the Fourteenth Amendment. The Colfax Massacre happened on April 13, 1873, in the small town of Colfax, Louisiana. It was a fight between blacks and whites, and about 150 blacks and three whites died in it. The massacre was an aftermath of the hotly contested Louisiana governor's race of 1872, which raised racial tensions.

As a result of the massacre, ninety-seven white men were arrested and charged with violation of the U.S. Enforcement Act of 1870 (also known as the Ku Klux Klan Act). They were convicted of conspiring to deprive those blacks of their constitutional rights. Their convictions were appealed, and, in 1876, the Court vacated convictions of Cruikshank and other whites who had been involved in the massacre. The Court vacated those convictions because it decided that the Fourteenth Amendment's enforcement clause was meant to protect individuals from actions by a State and not from actions of other individuals.

In this case the Court criticized indictments for not enumerating the crimes being indicted and for not demonstrating that those crimes were committed because of race. It found that the charges were so vague that those men indicted had been deprived of due process.

In the decision in this case, the Court ruled that the right to peaceable assembly was a natural right, which preceded the adoption of the Constitution, rather than a right granted by it. The First Amendment forbad Congress to abridge the right to assemble, but the First Amendment "was not intended to limit the powers of the state governments in respect to their own citizens, but to operate on the National government alone."

The view that the Bill of Rights applied only to the U.S. government was held by federal courts into the 20th century. In 1922, in Prudential Insurance Company of America v. Cheek, the Court reaffirmed this view. The case concerned a Missouri law that required corporations to give employees leaving its employ a letter stating the nature and duration of service and reason for leaving. The Court ruled that "The Federal Constitution imposes no restriction on the states protective of freedom of speech, or liberty of silence, or the privacy of individuals or corporations."

Since then the Supreme Court has gradually decided that the Bill of Rights apply to State legislation. It, thereby, reversed more than 130 years of its decisions regarding the first 10 amendments to the U.S. constitution. This new Court doctrine is known as "incorporation". With its new incorporation doctrine the Court gradually found that various portions of the Bill of Rights are applicable to state and local governments, because of wording in the Fourteenth Amendment and the Fifteenth Amendment. Most portions of these amendments are, as a result, now enforced against state governments.

When ratified, in 1791, the 5th Amendment to the Constitution guaranteed that persons charged in U.S. courts shall not be subject to double jeopardy. That meant that no one would be tried twice for the same crime in U.S. courts. At that time, it applied only to the U.S. However, the Supreme Court, in Benton v. Maryland, in 1936, decided that it also applies to the States.

The Supreme Court has since ruled that a person can be tried in a state and a federal court for the same crime. Since 1847, the Court has decided that state governments and the U.S. are separate sovereigns and trial for the same crime in both jurisdictions is not double jeopardy. This is known as the Supreme Court's Dual Sovereignty doctrine.

This means that, if a person is charged with breaking both a state and a U.S. law by one action, he may be tried for the crime in the relevant state court and in a U.S. court. Additionally, evidence and testimony presented by a prosecutor or defense lawyer in a trial in one system may be used against the defendant in the other.

Additionally, although second prosecutions for the same offense are forbidden, a person may be prosecuted for a lesser offense included in the charge for which he was already tried. For example, if a person is tried and acquitted of murder, he may later be tried again for manslaughter in both state and U.S. courts.

In Palko v. Connecticut, in 1937, the Supreme Court ruled against applying to the states the federal double jeopardy provisions of the Fifth Amendment. In its decision it laid the basis for the idea that some freedoms in the Bill of Rights, including the First Amendment's right to freedom of speech, are more important than others.

In this case Frank Palko had been charged with first-degree murder. He was convicted instead of second-degree murder and sentenced to life imprisonment. The state of Connecticut appealed and won a new trial; this time the court found Palko guilty of first-degree murder and sentenced him to death.

The Supreme Court was asked to decide if Palko's second trial for the same crime violated his protection from double jeopardy, which the Fifth Amendment guarantees, because this protection applies to the states because of the Fourteenth Amendment's due process clause.

The Supreme Court upheld Palko's second conviction. Its majority opinion also formulated principles that directed its actions for the next three decades. The Court said that some Bill of Rights guarantees, such as freedom of thought and speech, are fundamental, and that the Fourteenth Amendment's due process clause absorbed these fundamental rights and applied them to the states. It also ruled that protection from double jeopardy was not a fundamental right and is outside of constitutional protection.

In its 1969 decision, in Benton v. Maryland, the Court clearly overruled its decision in Palko. This time it held that the Double Jeopardy Clause of the Fifth Amendment applies to the states. and is an element of freedom protected by Due Process of the Fourteenth Amendment.

The dual sovereignty doctrine has also been used to allow successive prosecutions by two states for the same conduct, and to permit a U.S. prosecution after a conviction in an Indian tribal court for an offense stemming from the same conduct.

This is the current situation, and testimony and evidence presented by the prosecutor and defense in a federal criminal trial may be used against the defendant in a state criminal trial and vice versa.

Double jeopardy does not apply to civil court proceedings, which result from the same facts as does a criminal trial. However, evidence and testimony in a civil trial may be used against a defendant in a criminal trial and vice versa.

In a 2019 case, Justice Ruth Bader Ginsberg, in a dissenting opinion, wrote that successive prosecutions by state and U.S. legal systems is contrary to the purpose of the U.S. legal system, which should "operate as a double security for the rights of the people". She wrote that the U.S. and its states are "parts of one whole" and that the federal and state governments should be prevented from accomplishing together what neither government can do alone: which is to prosecute an ordinary citizen twice for the same offense.

In 1896, the Supreme Court ruled in Plessy v. Ferguson that racially segregated public facilities were legal, as long as the facilities for Black people and whites were equal.

In 1954, the Supreme Court ruled, in Brown v. Board of Education, that segregated public schools were inherently unequal. The decision was not based upon any law, but upon the psychological premise that segregated schools were "inherently unequal".

In 2005, the U.S. Supreme Court ruled that Connecticut could use its eminent domain power to take private land and transfer it to a private developer. The private land was owned by Susette Kelo, who had lived in a home on the property for more than 60 years. The lot on which her home stood was part of a comprehensive redevelopment plan created for the city of New London by the New London Development Corporation (NLDC), a nonprofit. The plan's purpose was to sell the properties to private developers in order to create new jobs and increase the city's tax revenue.

Kelo and several other owners sued the city in state court, arguing that the NLDC had misused its power of eminent domain. The eminent domain power is limited by the Fifth and Fourteenth Amendments to the United States Constitution. That amendment says, in part, that private property shall not be taken for public use, without just compensation". Under Section 1 of the Fourteenth

Amendment, this limitation is also imposed on the actions of U.S. state and local governments. Kelo and the other appellants argued that economic development, the stated purpose of the development corporation, did not qualify as public use.

The courts were asked to determine if a state using its eminent domain power to take private property and sell it to private developers to create jobs and increase tax revenue violates the Fifth Amendment's "public use" requirement?

The initial state court issued a split verdict, finding in favor of the landowners in one parcel and in favor of the NLDC in the other. Both landowners and NLDC then appealed the ruling to the Connecticut Supreme Court.

Their case was eventually laid before Connecticut's Supreme Court, which ruled in favor of all the proposed takings. Four judges dissented and found that the majority's opinion opened the door to the possibility of further use of eminent domain in any case where a new owner might use property more efficiently than the existing owner. They said that the NLDC had misused its power of eminent domain case in the Connecticut courts

The case was then appealed to the U.S. Supreme Court. where the property owners argued that economic development, the stated purpose of the NLDC, did not qualify as public use. They said that Connecticut had no right to use its eminent domain power to take their private property, because its plan to sell property that it took to private developers to create jobs and increase tax revenue violated the Fifth Amendment's "public use" requirement.

The U.S. Supreme Court ruled that Connecticut did not violate the Fifth Amendment and could use its eminent domain power to take private land and transfer it to a private developer for the "public purpose" of creating jobs and increasing tax revenue. In its opinion, the U.S. Supreme

Court noted a precedent created in Berman v. Parker, 348 U.S. 26 (1954), and Hawaii Housing Authority v. Midkiff, 467 U.S. 229 (1984). That case upheld a state's use of eminent domain when it took land from private individuals and sold to other private individuals. The U.S. Supreme Court upheld the takings, because the purpose of the eminent domain projects was held to promote public welfare in some form.

Four justices dissented from the majority in this case. They wrote that allowing the use of eminent domain in this case made it possible for eminent domain to be used in any case in which a new owner might use property more economically efficiently than the existing owner. They cited part of a decision by Justice Salmon P. Chase, in which he wrote, "An act of the Legislature (for I cannot call it a law) contrary to the great first principles of the social compact, cannot be considered a rightful exercise of legislative authority ... A few instances will suffice to explain what I mean...[A] law that takes property from A. and gives it to B: It is against all reason and justice, for a people to entrust a Legislature with such powers; and, therefore, it cannot be presumed that they have done it." (Calder v. Bull, 3 Dall. 386, 388 [1798])

The dissenting justices wrote that, "Today the Court abandons this long-held, basic limitation on government power. Under the banner of economic development, all private property is now vulnerable to being taken and transferred to another private owner, so long as it might be upgraded—i.e., given to an owner who will use it in a way that the legislature deems more beneficial to the public—in the process. To reason, as the Court does, that the incidental public benefits resulting from the subsequent ordinary use of private property render economic development takings "for public use" is to wash out any distinction between private and public use of property—and thereby effectively to delete the words 'for public use' from the Takings Clause of the Fifth Amendment."

In the case entitled Citizens United v. Federal Election Commission, the Court reversed century-old campaign-finance restrictions. The Court's new rule enables corporations and other outside groups to spend unlimited funds on elections. The decision greatly expanded the already great influence that wealthy donors, corporations, and special interest groups have in elections.

In this case, a conservative non-profit group called Citizens United was prevented by the FEC from promoting and airing a film critical of Hillary Clinton, the Democrats presidential candidate, too close to the 2008 Democratic primary elections. Advertising the film would have been a violation of the 2002 Bipartisan Campaign Reform Act, which prohibited any corporation, non-profit organization or labor union from making an "electioneering communication" within 30 days of a primary or 60 days of an election, or making any expenditure advocating the election or defeat of a candidate at any time.

Citizens United challenged the constitutionality of this law, and its case eventually reached the Supreme Court. The Court decided, in 2010, that the free speech clause of the First Amendment to the Constitution forbids the U.S. from limiting independent spending for political campaigns by corporations, labor unions, and other associations. The Court's decision invalidated the Bipartisan Campaign Reform Act of 2002, which forbad corporations and unions to spend their general funds on what it referred to as independent spending for "electioneering communication".

In doing so, the Court also overturned its 1990 decision, in Austin v. Michigan Chamber of Commerce, which had allowed a prohibition on election spending by incorporated entities, as well as a portion of its 2003 decision in

McConnell v. FEC, which approved restricted corporate spending on "electioneering communications". In these cases, the Court also ruled that spending restrictions helped to prevent corruption.

The Citizens United ruling effectively freed corporations, labor unions and incorporated non-profit organizations to spend money on electioneering communications and to directly advocate for the election or defeat of candidates

The ruling represented a sea change for campaign finance, for it allows unlimited election spending by corporations and labor unions. It created the basis for a U.S. Appellate Court decision, in the 2010 case Speechnow.org v. FEC, which ruled that contribution limits are unconstitutional as applied to individuals' contributions to SpeechNow. The Court's decision also authorized the creation of Independent Expenditure Committees, commonly known as Super PACs.

In Citizens United, the Court's majority decided that "independent political spending" did not present a substantive threat of corruption, provided it was not coordinated with a candidate's campaign. As a result, corporations can now spend unlimited funds on campaign advertising if they are not formally "coordinating" with a candidate or political party.

The ruling has ushered in massive increases in political spending from outside groups, dramatically expanding the already outsized political influence of wealthy donors, corporations, and special interest groups.

In the immediate aftermath of the Citizens United decision, analysts have tried to understand how the Supreme Court found that corporate spending on elections is free speech. However, the most significant outcomes of Citizens United have been the creation of super PACs, which empower the wealthiest donors, and the expansion of dark money through shadowy nonprofits that don't disclose their donors. As a result, Citizens United has resulted in massive political spending by special interest groups.

In a majority opinion, five justices held that the Bipartisan Campaign Reform Act's prohibition of all independent expenditures by corporations and unions violated the First Amendment's protection of free speech. The Court overruled its own decision in Austin v. Michigan Chamber of Commerce (1990), which had allowed a prohibition on election spending by incorporated entities, as well as a portion of McConnell v. FEC (2003), which had upheld restricted corporate spending on "electioneering communications".

The majority's decision created corporate or juridical personhood for corporate entities, which is separate from corporations' human personnel. It ruled that corporations have some of the legal rights and responsibilities that natural persons have.

The ruling effectively freed corporations (including incorporated non-profit organizations) to spend money on electioneering communications and to directly advocate for the election or defeat of candidates. In a dissenting opinion, Associate Justice John Paul Stevens argued that the Court's ruling represented "a rejection of the common sense of the American people, who have recognized a need to prevent corporations from undermining self-government."

The decision remains highly controversial. It created much public discussion and received strong support and opposition from various groups. Senator Mitch McConnell commended the decision, arguing that it represented "an important step in the direction of restoring the First Amendment rights". By contrast, President Barack Obama stated that the decision "gives the special interests and their lobbyists even more power in Washington".

The ruling represented a turning point on campaign finance. It allowed unlimited election spending by corporations and labor unions, and enabled Speechnow.org v. FEC, in 2010 to win a ruling by the U.S. District Court for the District of Columbia that contribution limitations cannot be constitutionally applied to SpeechNow.org and others that wanted to contribute to SpeechNow.org. The court ordered the Commission to permanently stop enforcing contribution limits. That resulted in the creation of Independent Expenditure Committees, more commonly known as Super PACs. It also created conditions for later rulings by the Court, including McCutcheon v. FEC, in 2014, which struck down other campaign finance restrictions. While the long-term legacy of this case remains to be seen, early studies by political scientists have concluded that Citizens United worked in favor of the electoral success of Republican candidates.

In June 2022, the Supreme Court ruled, in Dobbs v. Jackson Women's Health Organization, that women have no constitutional right to an abortion. Its decision overturned a 1973 decision, in Roe v. Wade, which ruled that the U.S. Constitution protects a pregnant woman's liberty to choose to have an abortion without excessive government restriction. The Roe v. Wade decision struck down many U.S. federal and state abortion laws. The ruling also overturned subsequent Supreme Court rulings that had reaffirmed women's right to abortions.

In Dobbs v. Jackson Women's Health Organization, the Court ruled that the Constitution does not give women a right to abortion. In this ruling, the Supreme Court negated its previous decisions in both Roe v. Wade and Planned Parenthood v. Casey. The Court also said that abortion must be decided in each state, by each state's voters. This means that each state may decide to ban abortions, which a majority of states now do.

For five decades Roe v. Wade had given women in the U.S. the right to abortions. The Supreme Court's ruling in Dobbs v. Jackson Women's Health Organization overturned Roe v Wade and ended five decades during which there was constitutional protection in the U.S. for sexual and reproductive health and rights. Overturning Roe v. Wade, by the Court, is a huge blow to women's human rights and gender equality. A result of this negation of women's rights to abortions under federal law is expected to cause legal chaos across the U.S.

This recent decision stirred up much negative public reaction against the Roman Catholic Church and fundamentalist Christians, which strove to get this decision and already had "trigger laws" in place in many states, which went into effect when the Supreme Court issued its decision.

One commentator noted that the same people that, based upon their religious beliefs, would forbid women to have abortions, condemn Taliban in Afghanistan for forcing people there to live according to the Taliban's religious beliefs.

In addition to reversing its previous rulings, the Court often choses to review subjects that appeal to its members, but about which they have little knowledge. For example, in June 2022 the Supreme Court ruled on regulatory power, which Congress gave to the Environmental Protection Agency (EPA), and struck down the EPA's standards for air and water quality. It said that "...it is not plausible that Congress gave EPA the authority to adopt on its own such a regulatory scheme. A decision of such magnitude and consequence rests with Congress itself, or an agency acting pursuant to a clear delegation from that representative body."

The case results from an EPA directive, in 2015, which would have required coal-burning power works to limit greenhouse gas emissions, which cause climate change. The directive was immediately challenged in court and never implemented. It is now invalid.

This Supreme Court decision restricts the EPA's tools to limit greenhouse gas emissions at a time when climate change is causing ice melts on Greenland, the Arctic, and Antarctica, and resulting in sea level rise. This ruling could have a serious impact on other federal regulatory agencies, all of which were created by Congress and ordered to regulate specific subjects.

In a dissenting opinion, Justice Elena Kagan wrote: "This is not the Attorney General regulating medical care, or even the CDC regulating landlord-tenant relations. It is the EPA (that's the Environmental Protection Agency, in case the majority forgot) acting to address the greatest environmental challenge of our time.

"The subject matter of the regulation here makes the Court's intervention more troubling. Whatever else this Court may know about, it does not have a clue about how to address climate change, And let's say the obvious: The stakes here are high. Yet the Court prevents congressionally authorized agency action to curb power plants' carbon dioxide emissions. The Court appoints itself—instead of Congress or the expert agency—the decision maker on climate policy. I cannot think of many things more frightening."

Then there are recent Court decisions in which the Court has begun to chip away at the First Amendment requirement that church and state be kept separate. In one recent decision, the Court allowed the use of tax money to pay tuition for children to attend parochial schools. Another allows a high school football coach to pray, on the field, with his school's team present, and a third favored a Christian group, which wanted to fly a flag with a cross on it on Boston's city hall, as a part of a diversity promotion program for that city's communities.

Reform

The Supreme Court has become a partisan über-legislature of nine justices with lifetime appointments that decide cases in keeping with their preferences and prejudices. The Court's routine interference with state and federal laws and regulations seriously undermines the separation of powers created by the Constitution.

The concentration of unrestrained, lifetime, judicial power in the hands of nine individuals is dangerous and damaging to representative government and constitutional governance.

Furthermore, when laws and regulations are appealed to the Supreme Court, it applies universalist, egalitarian requirements for the country's 330 million residents. Decisions ignore local feelings, customs, and traditions and apply inflexible national norms.

Different reforms have been suggested, which would end congressional contention when there is a vacancy on the Court and would also make the Court more representative of the American public. The best suggestion is to eliminate life tenure; institute staggered, non-renewable terms; have the most senior justice on the Court become Chief Justice, during his or her final period on the Court; and to require that only the chief judge of each state's highest court be eligible to be appointed a justice of the U.S. Supreme Court.

If the Court continues to consist of nine justices, one could be appointed every two years and 81 days. When a new justice is appointed, the most senior justice would retire from the Court, and the next most senior justice would become Chief Justice for the next two years and 81 days. These changes would significantly lessen the vicious political discord that happens when someone is nominated to the Court and when a new Chief Justice is nominated.

Eligibility for appointment to the Court should be limited to persons that are the chief judges of the highest court in each state. Nobody could be appointed from the same state as a justice currently on the Court, until head judges of all other states have served on the Supreme Court. This would give the Court the benefit of members that have better understandings of and respect for regional values than does the present nomination process. In this way, views from across the U.S. would be reflected in the Court's decisions.

If a justice died or was forced to retire for health or other reasons, that justice would be replaced, for the duration of his state's tenure on the Court, by the senior judge on his or her state's highest court. If the most senior judge on a state's highest court refused the chance to serve on the Supreme Court, then the next most senior judge on that state's highest court could join the Supreme Court.

This arrangement would also negate the need to appoint a Chief Justice. In its stead, the most senior justice on the Court, according to appointment date, would become Chief Justice for two years and 81 days. At the end of that two-year-81-day term, that Chief Justice would leave the Court permanently and be succeeded by the next most senior justice. This would remove the prize of Chief Justice from political contention, for each justice would eventually serve as Chief Justice without presidential appointment being required.

Judges would become eligible to serve on the Court according to the alphabetical sequence of their states' names. There would be no Senate hearings and Senate approval of new members. Since candidates lie and dissemble in the current system when questioned by senators, nothing would be lost, and fractious Senate hearings would be eliminated.

Setting the term for a justice at 10 years, with one replaced every two years and 81 days would end the ability of presidents to nominate persons that agree with their agenda.

Because the Constitution states that "The Judges, both of the supreme and inferior Courts, shall hold their Offices during good Behaviour," it will require a constitutional amendment to set term limits. Congress would enact this amendment and send it to the states to ratify.

Naming seasoned justices from state high courts to the U.S. Supreme Court would make the U.S. Supreme Court more representative of the States and their citizens. It would also do away with hearings at which persons nominated to the Court avoid giving meaningful answers, give evasive answers, and outright lie under oath in order not to reveal their political and social views.

Laws that Congresses pass are one-size-fits-all for 330 million U.S. residents that live in a geographical area that stretches from the Arctic Ocean into the Caribbean Sea, and from the Atlantic Ocean to 2,521 miles west of San Diego in the Pacific Ocean. Congressional laws are insensitive to the different regional cultural, traditional, ethnic, and linguistic traditions of various places and communities. This is particularly true of politically sensitive issues and social issues. By appointing the highest-ranking members of state high courts to the Supreme Court, some reasonable consideration for regional values should be included in the Court's considerations and rulings.

Successive Congresses have contributed to Supreme Court activism, by spending much of their time contending about how to spend each year's federal budget. They have no time in which to write rules to implement laws that they enact. They pay great attention to special interests, which want some of that money, and campaign contributions seem intimately connected with congressional appropriations.

Congress has little interest or time left in which to deal with politically contentious issues or to write regulations to implement laws, which they pass. They delegate that task to anonymous civil servants at regulatory agencies (such as EPA, FCC, IRS, and FDA), to write those regulations, which implement laws.

In addition to term limits for Supreme Court justices, the U.S. Supreme Court should be moved from Washington, D.C., to a place near the Rockies eastern edge in eastern Colorado or southern Wyoming. That would move the judicial branch of the federal government away from the eastern edge of the continent. It would also emphasize for Court members that there is more to the U.S. than Washington, D.C., and its suburbs.

By physically removing the Court from proximity to the legislative and executive branches it would also emphasize that the judicial branch is separate from them. An extra result would be that it would remove the justices, for part of each year, from cocktail parties and conventions in and near Washington, D.C., when the Court is in session, and enable them to concentrate on their work.

There are also 13 U.S. Courts of Appeal, each of which has three judges. Persons appointed to these courts should be judges from state appeals courts in the states that are in each U.S. appeals court's district. Appeals court judges should be appointed for a limited time, say ten years and not be re-appointed. State judges could become eligible to serve on the Court according to the alphabetical sequence of their states' names. There would be no Senate hearings and Senate approval of new members. This would put on those appeals courts persons familiar with the population, its customs and traditions in the geographical areas for which they adjudicate cases.

Finally, the arrangement for placing persons into U.S. District Court judgeships should be somewhat similar to that for appointing them to U.S. appeals courts. Persons named to U.S. District Court judgeships should be sitting judges on a state court in the state in which that district lies. As with appointments to U.S. appeals courts and the Supreme Court, appointments should be for a limited term.

Summary

The U.S. Supreme Court has made itself the senior legislative body of the United States' government. Originally, its legitimacy came from faithfully interpreting laws passed by Congress and adhering to the Constitution, as amended. For decades, the Court has digressed from the role assigned it by the Constitution and has become the supreme U.S. legislative branch. It strikes down laws, and rewrites laws and regulations to suit the will of its contemporary members. As a result, it has become highly political and contentious. It has also reversed its own decisions more than 300 times, reflecting the preferences or prejudices of its members.

An amendment to the U.S. Constitution is needed to remedy this and return the Court to its original tasks.

In addition to limiting members of the Court to one ten-year term, it should require that Court members, when appointed to the Court, must be chief judges of the highest court in their state. It should furthermore stipulate that the senior member of the U.S. Supreme Court shall serve as chief justice for two years and 81 days, and be succeeded as chief justice by the next most senior member when he or she finishes his or her 10-year term. In addition, the amendment should stipulate that state high-court senior judges shall join the Supreme Court in alphabetic order by state.

Placing senior, state, high-court judges on the Supreme Court would modify the Court's geographical representation, cultural view, and societal experience. It would also eliminate presidents' ability to "pack" the Court with partisans of their viewpoints. This procedure would remove the Court from the midst of politics where it is currently mired. It would also end contentious congressional hearings of presidential nominees to the Court and to the Chief Justice's position.

After an amendment is written and approved by Congress and sent to the states to approve, Congress should move the Court from the highly political environment of Washington DC, to a place just east of the Rockies, possibly in eastern Colorado or southern Wyoming. This would enable justices to pay more attention to their work and less to giving speeches at conventions and law schools.

The author

Norman Philip Black has served as a U.S. Navy Journalist, in the western Pacific; reported for United Press International and edited copy for Associated Press, both in New York City; and reported, in New Jersey, for the Newark Evening and Sunday News. He later worked in corporate public relations. His news reports, commentaries and features have appeared internationally. He has a B.A. and M.S. in Education, from Wagner College, and an M.S. in Journalism from Columbia University's Graduate School of Journalism.

www.ingramcontent.com/pod-product-compliance
Lightning Source LLC
Chambersburg PA
CBHW050307220526
45465CB00002B/864